DON'T PICK UP THE

BABY

OR YOU'LL SPOIL

the Child

—— AND OTHER ——

OLD WIVES'

TALES

ABOUT PREGNANCY
AND PARENTING

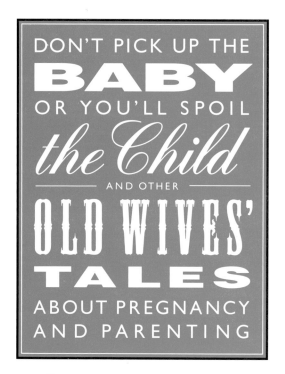

DON'T PICK UP THE BABY OR YOU'LL SPOIL *the Child* AND OTHER OLD WIVES' TALES ABOUT PREGNANCY AND PARENTING

COLLEEN DAVIS GARDEPHE & STEVE ETTLINGER

FOREWORD BY NIELS LAUERSEN, M.D., Ph.D.

ILLUSTRATIONS BY KAREN SMIDTH

Chronicle Books · San Francisco

Printed in Hong Kong.

Library of Congress Cataloging in Publication Data
Ettlinger, Steve.
 Don't pick up the baby or you'll spoil the child & other old wives' tales about pregnancy and parenting/Colleen Davis Gardephe and Steve Ettlinger.
   p.   cm.

 ISBN 0-8118-0242-6
  1. Pregnancy—Miscellanea.
 2. Infants—Care—Miscellanea.
 I. Gardephe, Colleen Davis.
 II. Title.
 RG525.E77   1993
 618.2'4—dc20   92-1600
                    CIP

Conceived and edited by Ettlinger Editorial Projects
Book and cover design: Karen Smidth
Composition: Words & Deeds

Distributed in Canada by Raincoast Books, 112 East Third Avenue, Vancouver, B.C. V5T 1C8

10 9 8 7 6 5 4 3 2 1

Chronicle Books
275 Fifth Street
San Francisco, CA 94103

EDITOR'S NOTE

For the purposes of this book, the newborn period is a baby's first month and infancy the first six months. Toddlerhood extends from fifteen months or so to age three; a child is then termed a pre-schooler until he enters kindergarten. The general term baby is often used during the first three years, but as we all know, a child can be his mother's "baby" all the days of his life.

The information in this book has been reviewed by a panel of physicians but it is not intended to substitute for the knowledge and advice of your own health care provider. Whenever you have any concerns or questions about your health or the health of your child, consult your doctor or other health care professional.

CONTENTS

To Paul and Tess, and Gusty and Dylan,
who helped us discover the joy and
wonderment of pregnancy and parenthood.

ACKNOWLEDGMENTS

WE WOULD LIKE TO EXTEND a warm thanks to the doctors, nurses, psychiatrists, and dieticians, among the many dozens, who shared their expertise with us, in particular: Rosemary Diulio, parent educator at the Maternity Center Association, in New York City; Dr. Esther Wender, pediatrician; Dr. Paul Dworkin, pediatrician; Jo Ann Heslin, registered dietician and coauthor of *No-Nonsense Nutrition for Your Baby's First Year;* Sally Wendkos Olds, child development expert and coauthor of *The Complete Book of Breastfeeding*; Dr. Jonathan Scher, obstetrician and author of *Preventing Miscarriage: The Good News*; Dr. Marjorie Szeto, obstetrician; Dr. David Fassler, child psychiatrist and author; Dr. William Meyers, pediatrician; Dr. Robert Mendelson, pediatrician; Dr. Steve Shelov, professor of pediatrics; and Dr. Mark Widome, pediatrician.

We would also like to thank the following health care professionals for reviewing the manuscript for this book: Dr. Susan Spitz, family physician and journalist; Dr. John Murashige, family physician; and Denise Joncich, obstetrical nurse.

Our sincere gratitude goes to Carol Murashige for her assistance in preparing the manuscript. And finally, we'd like to thank our editor at Chronicle Books, Jay Schaefer, for his enthusiastic support of this project as well as his insightful editing.

FOREWORD

"ANY QUESTIONS TODAY?" I asked one of my pregnant patients. "Yes," she said. I thought she might be concerned about her blood pressure, but instead, she surprised me.

"My friends tell me that if you gain a lot of weight in your face when you're pregnant, you're going to have a girl. If you're going to have a boy, you're only heavy in the middle. Since my face is fat, I think the baby's a girl. What do you think?" She waited for my reply.

I certainly did not know whether her baby would be a boy or girl based on her theory of weight distribution, but I was amused by her "words of wisdom." Hers was one of many humorous, harmless aphorisms about pregnancy and childbirth that I hear every day. The homespun advice expectant and new mothers receive is always well-meaning, and often quite comforting. I have found, however, that certain maxims that have been passed from generation to generation can mislead a woman at a time when she is trying to be particularly careful about everything she does.

That's why I was so pleased that Steve Ettlinger and Colleen Davis Gardephe decided to write this book. Here is a way for expectant and new parents to remain clearheaded. While I find it charming to hear about an old-fashioned way of finding out the sex of an unborn baby, it is worrisome to learn that unfounded advice about diet and exercise during pregnancy, and about aspects of childbirth and parenting, can be taken to heart. For instance, I recommend swimming as an excellent form of exercise during pregnancy, but the old wives' tale is that a pregnant woman should never swim in water above her waist. Steve and Colleen have separated the myths from the facts in their book and performed a valuable service in doing so.

Expectant and new parents should follow the advice of their doctors and other health care practitioners first and foremost. And asking their doctors about whether the advice they hear through word of mouth should be taken seriously still remains the best policy. With *Don't Pick Up the Baby*, women now have another source of good information, one they can carry with them. No appointment necessary.

NIELS H. LAUERSEN, M.D., PH.D.

INTRODUCTION

YOU ANNOUNCE THAT you're expecting a baby and suddenly your stomach becomes public property—everyone starts telling you what to do and what to expect, spewing out old superstitions and homespun wisdom with the certainty of a prophet. "Eat for two." "If your stomach's pointy, it's a boy." "First babies are usually late." Your every move is watched and analyzed to see that you're promoting the health and well-being of your baby.

The trouble is you're not sure if you should be listening or laughing. Even if you're a genius, you're likely to be a little gullible when it comes to your own child, especially when the advice comes from experienced parents. You care more about the health of your baby-to-be than you have cared about anything else in the world, so when people talk about her (throughout the book we alternate indiscriminately between male and female pronouns), you listen. You wonder if any of these sayings might be true.

Well, some are, though most are not. Some are half-true, mixing just the right amount of familiar disinformation and worry to sound tantalizingly factual.

Giving birth offers no reprieve. Then you're beseiged with unsolicited advice and predictions about parenting and your child's development. "Spare the rod, spoil the child!" "Let him cry; he's just exercising his lungs!" "Push a child to walk too early, and she'll be bowlegged!"

Some of these old wives' tales have persisted for thousands of years. The oldest medical records, which were kept by the Egyptians and date back to 1350 B.C., indicate that women tried to predict the sex of their offspring by moistening bags of barley and wheat with their urine. If the barley sprouted, a girl was thought to be due; if wheat grew, a boy was expected; and if neither germinated, the woman was not pregnant. The ancient Greeks contributed many other myths that are still popular today, and sex determination remains one of the favorite topics of soothsayers, perhaps because with fifty-fifty odds, people can still predict the gender correctly half the time. So despite the development of new medical tests such as amniocentesis, that can accurately determine the sex of the baby, the old theories flourish.

Why do the superstitions and myths persist in this age of modern technology? Some people will simply repeat the familiar advice that they themselves have heard, unsure—and not really remembering—whether it proved to be accurate or not. Some people figure if everyone is saying the same thing, then it must be true. Other people seem to believe that it is the act of giving advice itself that is comforting and helpful, whether or not the specifics of the advice are true all the time. And some people pass on old superstitions and myths not because they are true but because they are so funny or outlandish.

But when it comes to spreading these myths, people are also tying in to one of the most basic of all human experiences, one that has been shared and examined by every culture: birth. And for all our advancement in science, there is still much that is unknown about pregnancy and birth, child development and parenting. We still don't know, for example, what exactly triggers the onset of labor, or how much of a child's development is influenced by heredity as opposed to environment—the great "nature versus nurture" debate.

For the authors of this book, these old wives' tales have both a personal and professional significance. Ever since Steve, a writer and editor, took his baby outside for the first time and his older neighbor admonished him, "Don't pick up the baby every time he cries or you'll spoil him!" Steve knew he had to do this book. And when he found that Colleen, who is also a writer and editor and whose daughter was born only one month earlier than Steve's son, had already written on this subject, fate was sealed. The book was on.

We hope this book will help you sort through some of the myths and tales you will undoubtedly hear during this exciting and tumultuous time in your life. Of course, you should consult your health care professional about your serious questions.

In the meantime, here's *our* unsolicited advice: Learn from the tales that are true, laugh at those that are fun, and discard the rest. But most of all, enjoy your baby and relish your time together.

PREGNANCY

I

"*Babies are such a nice way to start people.*"

—DON HEROLD

SEX DETERMINATION

Hold a needle on a string in front of your stomach;
if it moves in a circle, you're having a girl. If it stays
still, you'll have a boy.

THIS LITTLE TEST is often performed on a pregnant
woman in a group setting, at work or at a party. Onlookers
gather round, eager to hear the proclamation "you're having
a boy," or "it's going to be a girl." While this test may be great
fun, its results have no merit. The movement of a needle can
in no way predict the sex of the baby.

If your nose grows larger, you're having a girl.

A NUMBER OF old wives' tales about pregnancy suggest that
girl babies sap their mother's beauty, so a woman is supposed
to look better when she's carrying a boy. In reality, there's no
link between the sex of the baby and the appearance of the
mother. Many women experience facial changes during pregnancy, however, including swelling of the nose. Increased es-
trogen levels heighten the flow of blood to the mucous
membranes, and as these membranes expand, so does
the nose, no matter what gender the baby is.

If you're carrying high, you'll have a boy.

If your stomach is pointy and it looks like you're carrying a watermelon, then it's a boy.

When your protruding stomach resembles a basketball, then it's a girl.

HOW A PREGNANT WOMAN carries her baby depends on a number of factors: the position of the baby, the shape of her pelvis, the tone of her abdominal muscles, and her posture, for example. If her abdominal muscles are lax, she may carry lower and jut out more. First-time mothers tend to carry higher than veteran moms, whose muscles are often weaker. The sex of the fetus, however, plays no role in how a woman carries her baby.

16

If you don't get morning sickness, you're having a boy.

BETWEEN ONE-THIRD and one-half of all pregnant women experience some degree of "morning sickness," nausea and vomiting that often occurs in the morning but can last all day long. According to folk wisdom, women who are carrying boys don't experience this nausea because the male hormone testosterone, which is produced in the gonads of the male fetus, protect her from it.

While physicians haven't completely ruled out the possibility that a woman's testosterone levels play a role in combatting nausea, most believe that relaxin, a hormone that's produced by the mother and isn't related to the sex of the fetus, is the real culprit behind morning sickness. Furthermore, all you have to do is poll several mothers of boys about this testosterone theory, and you'll undoubtedly find some who refute it, noting that they, too, experienced the morning sickness blues.

17

Lie on your right side after intercourse in order to have a boy.

THIS MYTH HAS PERSISTED since the ancient Greeks, when Hippocrates reportedly believed that boys developed on the right side of a woman's uterus and girls on the left. His students told would-be parents that in order to conceive a boy, the woman should lie on her right side after intercourse. But as the birds and the bees lesson says, the sex of the baby is determined at the moment of conception, when the father's sperm fertilizes the mother's egg.

Since the mother's egg always contains an X chromosome and the father's sperm an X or a Y chromosome, the sex of the baby is determined when a sperm carrying either a Y chromosome fertilizes the X egg, resulting in an XY (male), or when a sperm carrying an X chromosome fertilizes the egg, yielding an XX (female). Whether the fertilized egg attaches to the left or right side of the uterus makes no difference to the sex of the embryo.

If the fetus is active, it's a boy. If it's calm, it's a girl.

IF YOU THINK there's a linebacker working out in your uterus, you may be surprised when you find out a dainty little girl was causing all that ruckus. While most male toddlers are more physically active than their female play dates, this difference between the sexes doesn't hold true when they're in the womb.

A woman's ability to detect fetal activity depends on a number of factors. Veteran mothers are more likely to sense the earliest signs of life or "quickening" before first-time moms. Slender women may feel the fetus' movements more readily than those who weigh more. And a fetus' swift kicks and knock-out punches are less apt to register if it is facing inward.

19

A fast heart rate means you're having a girl; a slow heart rate means you're having a boy.

THOUGH THIS COMMONLY held, long-standing theory may sound scientific, it's not. The heart rate of a fetus generally ranges from 120 to 160 beats per minute in utero regardless of its gender. When a fetus is resting its heart rate slows down, and when the fetus is active the rate accelerates, just like mom's does.

LABOR AND DELIVERY

First babies are usually late.

TRUE, IN THE SENSE that just over half (60 percent) arrive after their due date. Only 5 percent of first babies arrive on their projected due date, while 35 percent arrive early. One way to calculate your due date is to take the first day of your last period and add forty weeks (or nine months and seven days) to it. Doctors usually use a different approach to arrive at a due date: add one year from the first day of your last period, subtract three months, and then tack on seven days.

The timing is tied to the length of your menstrual cycle. If your cycles usually last twenty-eight days, you're more likely to deliver close to your due date. If your cycles are longer, there's a greater chance you'll be late, and if they're shorter, you're more likely to deliver before the due date.

Don't dance while you're pregnant or you'll have your baby early.

DANCE AWAY, unless your doctor has advised you not to because of complications in your pregnancy or because you are at high risk for miscarriage. As with any exercise, you need to avoid fatigue, overexertion, and becoming short of breath or overheated. It's best to limit any period of aerobic activity, including dancing, to twenty-minute intervals. Always start with a warm-up period and conclude with a cool down of slower-paced exercises. To minimize leg cramping, don't point your toes when stretching or dancing. Choose music with a moderate tempo so you don't overdo it.

Ideally, a pregnant woman's heart rate should stay below 140 beats per minute during any physical exertion so that the baby's oxygen supply isn't diminished. And she should drink plenty of fluids so she stays well hydrated.

21

A sudden fright or scare will trigger delivery.

IF EVERY FRIGHT or scary movie triggered delivery, plenty of eager moms-to-be would be running out in their ninth month to the nearest video store to rent a horror film. A fleeting stressful moment isn't likely to trigger delivery or harm the fetus. A well-balanced diet and plenty of rest can usually offset the effects of daily stress for most pregnant women.

More babies are born when there's a full moon.

22

ASK A MIDWIFE, obstetrician, or obstetrical nurse about this and they're likely to note that labor floors are always full when the barometric pressure is low—just before a full moon, or during a hurricane, snowstorm, or tornado. It's thought that the gravitational pull associated with low barometric pressure causes the bag of waters to break. While this theory may be fun to ponder, not all studies support it.

Drinking raspberry tea will help induce labor.

SOME HEALTH CARE PROVIDERS believe raspberry tea promotes better contractions during labor. It will not *start* labor, however, and most doctors and midwives don't want their patients trying any such home brews. Some herbal teas, including cohosh, comfrey, and goldenseal, are not recommended during pregnancy.

Castor oil will speed delivery.

MIDWIVES OFTEN ENCOURAGE the use of castor oil to start contractions when a woman's membranes have ruptured but she hasn't gone into labor. This remedy reportedly works about half the time. Using castor oil on your own, however, is not recommended: It should only be taken on the advice of your health care practitioner, who can tell if you're a good candidate for castor oil and can recommend the proper dosage.

Delivery is a lot easier the second time around.

FORTUNATELY, THIS generalization holds true for most women. Labor and delivery lasts fourteen hours, on average, for first-timers, while the birthing process takes an average of only six or seven hours with baby number two and may decline slightly more with each successive child. After five children, some women's abdominal muscles may lose considerable tone, so labor may become more difficult again.

Since women who already have given birth know what to expect, they often do feel more confident and less nervous during second and third deliveries. But of course, the baby's size and position as well as the mother's overall health and well-being will determine the length and difficulty of labor.

Once a caesarean, always a caesarean.

NOT TOO LONG AGO, this was the standard adhered to in delivery rooms, but in the 1980s vaginal births after caesarean (VBAC) became more common. Today, 50 to 80 percent of women who have had C-sections can have successful vaginal births. They must meet a number of criteria to qualify for VBAC, including the following: Their incision must have been a low transverse cut on the uterus and not the less common high vertical cut (check with your doctor to see which one you had); their pregnancies must be normal; and they need to begin labor within twelve to twenty-four hours after the rupture of their membranes.

24

If your mother had an easy pregnancy and delivery, so will you.

IF BOTH YOU AND YOUR MOTHER have a normal, adequate pelvis, then she may have been and you may be blessed with an easy delivery. And while it's true that certain parallels, like rapid labor and early delivery, may exist, many other factors play a role in how smoothly a pregnancy or delivery goes so that heredity is not considered a key determinant. The size and position of the baby, along with your diet, lifestyle, and attitude, will all play greater roles than heredity in determining the ease or difficulty of your pregnancy and delivery. Besides, medicine's approach to childbirth has changed dramatically since your mother's time.

HEALTH AND LOOKS
OF MOM & BABY-TO-BE

*If you have a lot of heartburn during pregnancy,
your baby will be born with a lot of hair.*

MOMS CARRYING LITTLE BALDIES inside are just as likely to experience heartburn during pregnancy. Physical changes in the mother's body—not the baby's—are the primary causes of heartburn. The mother's increased progesterone helps relax the muscles between the stomach and the esophagus, allowing stomach fluid to flow more readily into the esophagus. Since the esophagus isn't coated with the same protective lining as the stomach, the acid fluids irritate the area. Heartburn is more likely to occur in the second and third trimesters, when the uterus enlarges and pushes the stomach and its contents up.

To minimize the likelihood of heartburn, avoid greasy, spicy foods, eat smaller meals, sip milk, and wait at least thirty minutes after eating before lying down. Chewing gum after meals may help. Women with severe heartburn should ask their doctor about taking an over-the-counter antacid.

Eat for two!

THIS TIME-HONORED ADAGE is true but often misconstrued. You must remember that the second person you're eating for is very tiny and only requires three-hundred calories of food a day. You should only consume an additional three-hundred to five-hundred calories a day while you're pregnant, and the foods you choose should be rich in iron, protein, calcium, and vitamins A, B, and C. Think of the food you eat as fuel for your baby's all-important tasks of growing and getting stronger and healthier. It is now recommended that women gain twenty-five to thirty-five pounds during pregnancy. Thin women and those carrying twins may need to gain more, while heavier women can gain less.

26

Once you adopt a baby, you're sure to get pregnant.

THIS CAUSALITY IS not only wrong, it can also be an irritating assertion to adoptive parents who choose adoption so they can bring a child into their lives to love and nurture, not so they can finally achieve pregnancy.

While many women who adopt children later get pregnant, it's highly unlikely that the adoption cured their infertility. The stress of trying repeatedly to conceive can exacerbate some physical problems, though stress alone rarely causes infertility. It's more likely that time, chance, fertility drugs, or surgery helped them to conceive.

All pregnant women crave pickles and ice cream,
generally during the middle of the night.

THE "HONEY, IT'S 4 A.M. and I want some ice cream!"
caricature of pregnant women may be more fiction than fact,
but cravings for foods that are sweet or salty are fairly common
during pregnancy. They seem to be triggered by a rise in a
woman's progesterone level.

The theory that the cravings are signs that your body needs
the minerals in those foods may be true if you have a burning
desire for liver and broccoli, but if visions of potato chips and
candy bars are dancing in your head, then unfortunately this
notion doesn't hold. If you crave food that's nutritious, go
ahead and indulge yourself. Even a little ice cream, particularly the low-fat variety, won't hurt and will give your body
some of the calcium it needs. But if you're craving potato
chips, look for healthier alternatives, like popcorn or unsalted
pretzels, or limit your intake to a few at a time. Middle-of-the-
night cravings are often thought to be pleas for attention, so
you may want to think about what it is you really crave and
communicate this need to your partner.

If you catch a cold during pregnancy, you'll keep it for the duration.

YOU MAY NOT KEEP the cold until you deliver, but it will seem hard to shake. Pregnant women often complain of nasal congestion because the blood vessels in the nose dilate, giving them a stuffed-up feeling. To combat their colds and stuffiness, women can drink plenty of fluids and use a humidifier or vaporizer to help clear their nostrils. It's best to avoid nasal sprays and cold medications during pregnancy.

You can teach your baby in the womb.

28

NEWBORNS CAN recognize television soap operas, children's stories, and music their moms listened to while they were in the womb. But can they learn the alphabet or a poem in utero? No. While they can perceive speech patterns in the womb, they can't comprehend words or meanings. Not even Einstein was born reciting the ABCs.

It's bad luck to buy anything for the baby before it is born.

THIS SUPERSTITION harks back to a time when childbirth was riskier. Many ethnic and religious groups, however, hold on to this belief, maintaining that the purchase of furniture or clothing beforehand will jinx the outcome of the delivery. Clearly, mothers- and fathers-to-be need to follow their instincts in this area and do whatever makes them feel most comfortable.

You won't get stretch marks if you rub your stomach with oil twice a day.

SINCE 90 PERCENT of all pregnant women get stretch marks, it's clear that no one has come up with a foolproof prevention or cure for them. Some women, however, believe they can minimize the pink squiggly lines on their breasts, thighs, and tummies by applying cocoa butter or vitamin E cream every day or by pouring oil into their baths. Lubricating the body will also help alleviate the itchiness that's common during pregnancy.

Stretch marks are generally caused by a rapid or dramatic increase in weight. To keep marks to the minimum, you can limit weight gain to twenty-five to thirty-five pounds and try to gain steadily. Including plenty of protein in your diet and firming abdominal muscles with regular exercise will also help ward off stretch marks, which are more likely to surface in blondes, overweight women, and first-time moms. After child-birth, stretch marks fade considerably but do not disappear completely.

29

Never swim in water above your waist or your baby will drown.

YOUR FETUS IS SAFELY cocooned in the amniotic sac
and won't be harmed in the least if you swim in deep water.
Swimming, in fact, is one exercise that's highly recommended
for pregnant women since it's easy on the joints and it's aerobic. Women are advised, however, to avoid swimming in water
that's rough, cold, or unclean. Chlorinated pools get a thumbs-
up from doctors, but they recommend that women rinse the
chlorine off soon after each swim.

Don't get your hair dyed or permed during pregnancy.

WHILE NO STUDIES have found a direct link between a mother's hair treatments and chromosomal abnormalities in her baby, research has shown that the chemicals in hair dyes can penetrate the scalp, enter the mother's bloodstream, and reach the fetus through the placenta.

To play it safe, health care providers recommend that women either avoid getting their hair dyed during pregnancy or choose natural coloring products, like henna. It's also best to hold off on dyes until the first trimester passes, since the baby's brain and nervous system are forming then. Hair treatments that coat the hair shaft rather than penetrate the scalp, like frosting and streaking, are safer bets. Perms are best avoided too, but some doctors note that if only the lower half of the hair is curled, the chemicals don't penetrate the scalp.

31

A hot bath will bring on a miscarriage.

WARM BATHS CAN HELP soothe tired muscles and relax a pregnant body. Luckily, they're considered safe throughout pregnancy until a woman's bag of water breaks, shortly before she goes into labor. The water temperature in a bath shouldn't be excessively hot, however, because a rise in a woman's body temperature can reduce the flow of blood to her baby. For that reason, hot tubs and saunas are also considered taboo.

Don't lie or sleep on your back or you'll hurt the baby.

32

MANY DOCTORS ENCOURAGE their pregnant patients to lie on their left sides as often as they can because doing so increases the flow of blood to the uterus and placenta. Sleeping on your side with a pillow under your hips or between your legs can help reduce the likelihood of hemorrhoids, improve circulation, and enhance kidney function. Lying on your back is generally not advised because it can cause backaches and it puts a lot of pressure on the major blood vessel that carries blood from your lower body to your heart. While you won't hurt your baby if you lie on your back for short periods of time, both of you will be better off if you sleep on your side.

You shouldn't jog when you're pregnant.

A JOGGER'S HEELS, knees, breasts, and back all take a beating, and for a pregnant woman whose ligaments and tendons are softer, breasts are larger, and center of gravity has shifted, the toll jogging takes on these body parts may be too great. A woman who was an avid runner before she became pregnant, however, can probably handle the stress, with the help of a good support bra and highly shock-absorbent running shoes.

Walking, swimming, and riding a stationary bike all help strengthen the muscles with less strain on the body than jogging, and for that reason make better exercise choices for most pregnant women. Moderate exercise during a problem-free pregnancy can help minimize lower back pain and leg cramps, and keep a woman fit and upbeat. It may also ease delivery and help her return to her prepregnancy weight more easily once the baby is born.

For every child, you will lose a tooth.

THOUGH IT'S NOT LIKELY that you'll sacrifice a tooth every time you give birth, the true hidden messages here are that women require more calcium during pregnancy and that they need to watch for dental problems. Calcium needs increase by 50 percent during pregnancy, from a Recommended Daily Allowance (RDA) of 800 milligrams to 1,200 milligrams. Calcium is necessary to fuel the growth of the fetus' heart, skeleton, muscles, and tooth buds. If you don't take in enough calcium, your fetus will start to deplete your own reserves, though from your bones, not your teeth. If you're unable to consume enough calcium through the foods you eat, you can ask your doctor about taking a calcium supplement. During pregnancy, a woman's saliva becomes more acidic, which may help promote tooth decay. Her gums are more likely to swell and bleed as well. The second trimester is often the best time for a pregnant woman to visit her dentist.

If a mother receives a sudden shock during pregnancy, her baby will be born with a birthmark.

If you eat strawberries during pregnancy, your baby will be born with a birthmark.

MORE THAN HALF of all newborns have some type of birthmark, but none of them originated because their mother was frightened or ate strawberries during pregnancy. The most common birthmarks, called "stork bites" or "salmon patches," are red areas on the neck, nose, and eyelids. These generally disappear by the time a baby is six to nine months old.

One-tenth of all babies have strawberry hemangiomas, most of which disappear by the time a child is five or six. Dark blue marks, or "Mongolian spots," on the baby's back and buttocks disappear more gradually and are generally gone by the time a child is seven or eight. Only birthmarks the color of port-wine are lasting.

Sex during pregnancy will hurt the baby.

ENJOYING AN ACTIVE SEX LIFE throughout pregnancy poses no danger to either the mother or the baby. The fetus is well protected inside the amniotic sac. Since the membranes of the amniotic sac can rupture at any time, however, some doctors advise couples to use condoms during the last four to eight weeks of pregnancy to minimize the risk of infection.

If you are considered a high-risk candidate for miscarriage or premature labor, you should check with your doctor about the safety of sex throughout your pregnancy.

Don't reach up or you'll strangle the baby with the umbilical cord!

36

THE MUSCLES INVOLVED in the lifting of your arm work independently of the fetus, which is safely ensconced in the amniotic sac. The position of the umbilical cord at birth has nothing to do with what the mother does or doesn't do during pregnancy. The cord is loosely draped around the baby's neck in approximately 25 percent of all births and can usually be slipped over the baby's head as soon as the head emerges from the birth canal.

MYTHS THAT NEED NO RESPONSE

The more macho the father is, the more likely the first child will be a girl.

If you have to shave your legs often when you're pregnant, the baby will be a girl.

If the brown line down your stomach ends at the top of your belly button, it's a boy; if it ends below your belly button, it's a girl.

Dream of a knife or a hatchet and you're expecting a boy. Dreams about spring or parties mean you're having a girl.

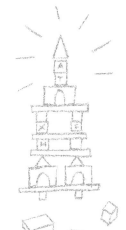

If you gain weight in your legs during pregnancy, according to the French, you're having a boy. If you gain weight in your face, a girl's on board, maintain the Italians.

If more freckles appear on a woman's pregnant body, a girl is on the way, according to Hippocrates.

A woman whose hair is shiny and bouncy during pregnancy is carrying a boy, Swedish folklore asserts. If her hair gets thin and straggly, then she's having a girl.

If you have a hankering for sweets, then it's a girl. Cravings for salty foods signify a boy.

If you conceived in the morning, you'll have a boy.

If the father sits on the roof near the chimney for seven hours, his next child will be a boy.

If the dad-to-be is a little jittery, then a girl's on the way. If he's cool as a cucumber, then a boy's due to arrive.

The sex of the baby will match that of the more vigorous lovemaking partner at the time of conception, according to the ancient Greeks.

39

If a north wind is blowing when fertilization takes place, then a boy is in the offing, Aristotle noted.

If someone drops a penny down your back and it lands tails, you're having a girl. If it's heads, you're going to have a boy.

If your firstborn says "mama" first, your next one will be a girl. If your firstborn says "dada" first, you'll have a boy next time.

Open all doors and drawers, spill out flour and sugar, and undo knots for easy labor.

Eat lasagna before delivery and your labor will last only four hours.

40

Drink a teaspoon of olive oil every day and your baby will slip right out.

If you scratch your stomach when pregnant, you'll get stretch marks.

Eat green beans during pregnancy and you won't get stretch marks.

Eat a lot of bread while you're pregnant so your baby will be smart.

Babies born with large ears are lucky, the English believe.

If the initials of a baby's name spell a word, the baby will be wealthy.

Babies born with large, wide mouths will grow up to be great singers.

41

PARENTING

2

"*Adam and Eve had many advantages,
but the principle one was that they escaped teething.*"

—MARK TWAIN

BREAST-FEEDING AND BOTTLE-FEEDING

Bottle-fed babies eat more and get fatter.
You can't overfeed a breast-fed baby.

THESE OBSERVATIONS MAY sometimes be true, but not always. The composition of breast milk, with the high-protein milk released first (fore milk) followed by the high-fat milk (hind milk), helps control a baby's consumption of fat and calories to some extent. In fact, the American Academy of Pediatrics recently called for the creation of new growth charts for breast-fed infants, noting that from the ages of six months to eighteen months, breast-fed babies tend to weigh less than those who are bottle-fed.

On the other hand, plenty of breast-fed babies look pretty roly-poly. If a mother nurses her baby constantly, even when he's just bored or cranky, he can be overfed. With bottle-fed babies, the risk of overfeeding comes when a parent encourages the baby to drain the bottle, even if he seemed full several ounces earlier. To avoid overfeeding a breast-fed or bottle-fed baby, follow his cues, stop feeding when he seems full, and offer some other form of comfort besides food when he seems bored or irritable.

Don't eat chocolate, tomatoes, strawberries, cabbage,
garlic, onions, or spicy foods while you're nursing or
your baby will cry all night.

BABIES ARE BREAST-FED all over the world, and their moms eat all different kinds of food; there just aren't universal rules or reactions for any one food. You don't need to eliminate any food from your diet unless your baby seems to have an adverse reaction to something you ate or drank. If, for example, your baby gets a tummyache or diarrhea four to six hours after you consumed a cup of yogurt and a glass of milk, she may be allergic to cow's milk. You can eliminate the suspected culprit from your diet for one or two weeks and see if the condition clears up. You can gradually add the suspected food back into your diet, because the baby's digestive system may become mature enough to handle it.

Foods that upset some babies include dairy products, eggs, wheat, peanut butter, fish, chocolate, citrus fruits, cabbage, broccoli, and caffeinated beverages. Spicy foods seldom pose a problem for babies.

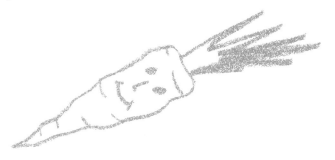

You can't breast-feed if your breasts are small.

YOU DON'T HAVE TO BE buxom to breast-feed. The size or shape of a breast has absolutely no impact on its ability to produce or dispense milk and to satisfy a hungry baby. The amount of fatty tissue surrounding your mammary glands determines the size of your breasts. Since this fatty tissue plays no role in the making or dispensing of milk, it doesn't matter one bit if your breasts are large or small. Breast-feeding is all a matter of supply and demand. The more your baby nurses, the more milk your body produces.

Breast-feeding will ruin your breasts.

NOT AT ALL. Any sagging of your breasts after delivery is actually attributable to heredity, age, poor support (going braless), or excessive weight gain during pregnancy. During pregnancy, your breasts will generally enlarge one cup size and will remain larger while you're breast-feeding and then return to their pre-pregnancy size soon after you wean your baby. Some nursing women find their breasts are larger after nursing, some say they're smaller, but most see no change at all. For women who don't nurse, the breasts generally return to the prepregnancy size in six to eight weeks, albeit a little softer than before.

45

Drinking beer or wine stimulates milk production.

NURSING MOTHERS MIGHT still enjoy an occasional cocktail, but recent studies have disproved the notion that alcohol stimulates their let-down reflex and yields more breast milk. Infants may actually consume less milk after their mothers drink alcohol. Nursing moms don't have to refrain from drinking altogether, however, since moderate amounts of alcohol leave the body in three or four hours. Moms can either express their milk beforehand or time their consumption accordingly. Heavy drinking, though, should be avoided since it can depress a baby's nervous system and make him drowsy.

You can't get pregnant when you're breast-feeding.

IF YOU DON'T WANT to have two back-to-back pregnancies, don't rely on breast-feeding as a form of birth control. It's true that nursing mothers generally resume ovulation later than moms who bottle-feed their babies, but there's no definitive way to know when ovulation will begin again.

For non-lactating mothers, ovulation generally resumes between four and eight weeks after delivery, while nursing moms may wait three to six months or longer before ovulation starts again. Most women have one sterile menstrual period that warns them they're about to ovulate, but some don't get this advance notice.

Once a mother starts menstruating again, she should stop nursing.

TWO MYTHS LIE BEHIND this assertion. One is that when a woman has her period, her milk will taste bad; the other is that the blood loss will leave her too weak to nurse. Neither of these theories is true. The *quality* of a woman's breast milk isn't affected by menstruation, and the blood loss during her period is minimal. It is true, however, that the hormonal changes that occur when she's menstruating can affect the *quantity* of her milk supply. To offset any decrease in supply, she can simply nurse more often.

Most nursing mothers resume menstruation within three to six months of delivery. Breast milk is considered the optimal source of nutrition during the first year of a baby's life.

47

If you're nervous when you nurse, your milk will turn sour.

BEING NERVOUS OR STRESSED out won't "sour" a woman's breast milk or have any impact on the quality of her supply. A woman who's tense or nervous, however, may find she produces less milk or has a harder time nursing. She can experiment with different ways to relax while she's nursing, such as lying down, propping up her feet, or listening to music. Eventually, she may find nursing relaxing in itself. During nursing, a woman's body releases prolactin, a hormone that has a calming effect.

48

You can't nurse during the first few days after delivery because there's no milk.

NOTHING COULD BE FURTHER from the truth. If this were so, all babies would starve. During the first one to five days after delivery, a woman's breasts secrete colostrum, an absolutely ideal first food for her baby. While it resembles mature breast milk in many ways, it's more watery, easier to digest, and contains more antibodies. It serves a number of important functions: It boosts the baby's infection-fighting capabilities; provides important nutrients; and acts as a laxative to clear out the baby's bowels. From about six days to two weeks after delivery, a woman's breasts produce transitional milk, and after that, the mature milk comes in.

Breast-fed babies don't get colic.

IF ONLY IT WERE that simple. Unfortunately, equal numbers of breast-fed and bottle-fed babies experience the daily crying bouts that characterize colic. The inconsolable sobbing generally extends for three or four hours a day and the condition lasts for about three months. About one in five babies develop colic, regardless of sex.

No one knows for sure what causes colic, but doctors believe that one-third of the cases stem from milk allergies. It seems that some bottle-fed babies can't tolerate the sugar or protein in cow's-milk formulas while some breast-fed infants react to the dairy products in their mothers' diets. Bottle-fed babies who are allergic to cow's milk can switch to a soy-based formula, while nursing mothers may want to avoid dairy products for one to two weeks to tell whether their children were reacting to them.

49

It's harder to get back to your prepregnancy weight if you're nursing.

WRONG. NURSING HELPS women return to their prepregnancy weight, in two ways: It burns up calories and fat stores, and it stimulates uterine contractions, which helps to shrink the uterus and strengthen the abdominal muscles. On the other hand, nursing women are advised not to diet too strenuously because cutting back dramatically can lessen their milk supply and release toxins into their bodies. For that reason, nursing mothers often hold on to the last ten pounds for a longer period of time than their non-nursing counterparts.

It's best to limit weight loss to no more than two and a half pounds a week during lactation and regard getting back into shape as a long-term process.

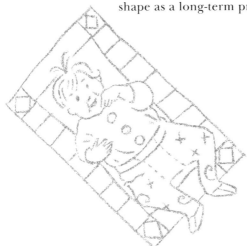

Bottle-fed babies develop closer relationships with their fathers, who can feed them.

DEVELOPING A CLOSE RELATIONSHIP with a baby goes well beyond feeding her. Fathers of babies who are breast-fed can hold and rock their babies, diaper and dress them, and sing and dance with them. Since breast milk is the best source of food for an infant, a father can be happy knowing his baby is getting the best. Once mother and baby have established their breast-feeding relationship, usually when the baby is around six weeks old, dad can feed the baby with relief bottles of breast milk or formula.

Breast-feeding prevents allergies.

51

THOUGH FEW REMEDIES are absolute, the antibodies in breast milk do seem to offer some protection against respiratory tract infections, food allergies, and some skin rashes.

Babies can't go back and forth between breast and bottle.

MANY BABIES GO BACK and forth between breast and bottle with apparent ease, though some babies are so discriminating they develop a strong preference for the softness of their mother's breasts or the ease with which they can get their milk from a bottle nipple. For a breast-fed baby who turns up his little nose at a bottle, mom can recruit her husband or mother to offer the bottle and experiment with an assortment of different nipples until they find one the baby likes. It's best to wait till a nursing baby is around six weeks old, when lactation is well established, to introduce a bottle. But don't wait too long. After four months a breast-fed baby is likely to vocalize his objections to the bottle loudly and clearly.

With a baby who rejects the breast once he's tried the bottle, a mother can try to breast-feed him when he's sleepy. He'll probably forget to reject the breast and may be willing to develop a nursing routine again.

FEEDING AND WEIGHT GAIN

All toddlers are picky eaters.

SOON AFTER HER FIRST birthday, a child may start to eat sparingly and erratically, which can drive her parents crazy. But her irregular eating habits are rarely cause for concern. For one thing, her body needs less fuel than it did during her first year of life, when she may have tripled her weight. Secondly, studies show that when young children are offered a variety of foods, they consume the proper amount of calories they require each day, somewhere between 740 and 1,300. They may eat very little at one meal and chow down at the next, but they'll take in what they need.

Nutritionists advise parents to offer children a wide range of healthy meal and snack choices, accept their changing day-to-day food preferences, and never force children to eat.

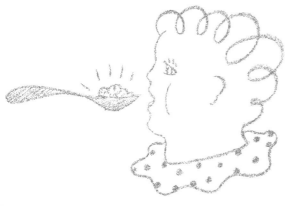

A baby will naturally outgrow his baby fat.

YOUR LITTLE CHERUB isn't likely to remain chubby the rest of his life. A number of studies suggest that a baby's weight on his first birthday has little to do with whether he will or won't be overweight later in life. A child's weight at the age of five or six is a better predictor of his future size.

A child's body has its highest level of fat, about 25 percent of his total weight, at the age of six or seven months, so it's no wonder that many babies this age look plump. Once a baby starts toddling, generally between twelve and fifteen months of age, he starts to lose his roly-poly appearance. And once his body lengthens during toddlerhood, he'll start to appear slimmer.

54

Chubby babies are healthier than thin babies.

IN PREVIOUS GENERATIONS, a chubby baby was considered the picture of health, probably with good reason. Thin babies were often underfed and malnourished. But the tide has turned and with malnutrition less of a problem today, heavier babies are no longer automatically considered healthier or less healthy than their thinner nurserymates. Today thin babies are usually just as healthy as chubby babies.

Breakfast is the most important meal of the day.

FOR CHILDREN, this axiom is doubly true. Breakfast skippers often don't do as well in school as those who take the time to eat. They have a harder time concentrating, are more prone to errors, and don't handle the repetitive aspects of learning math and reading as well.

The earlier a parent helps a child develop a routine that includes eating breakfast, the more likely it is to become a lifelong habit. Good breakfast choices include fruit and fruit juices, milk, eggs, bread, unsweetened cereal, yogurt, cheese, and lean meats.

Sugar makes a child hyperactive.

55

ON THE CONTRARY, sugar often makes a child feel sleepy. Several studies have refuted the long-held theory that sugar causes excitability in children. Foods that are high in sugar increase the level of the neurotransmitter serotonin in the brain, which has a calming, sleep-inducing effect on children. Since too much sugar can make a child lethargic and impede his ability to concentrate, school-aged children should particularly avoid sugar overloads at breakfast and lunch. Oftentimes it is the festivity and excitement of the party, rather than the sugar in the cake, that stimulates a child.

Cold milk will give a baby a tummyache.

A BABY WHO'S GIVEN cold milk is no more likely to experience stomach cramping than his playmate whose bottle is warmed. Food is warmed as it passes through the digestive tract, so nothing arrives in the belly ice cold. Most babies do like their milk served room temperature or warmer, though. What really upsets them is inconsistency—getting a warm bottle one day and a cold one the next.

Milk is necessary for growing bones.

MILK PROVIDES A CHILD with plenty of calcium, which is necessary for the development of strong bones, muscles, and teeth. The Recommended Daily Allowance (RDA) of calcium for a child under eleven is 800 milligrams, which can largely be met by the consumption of two eight-ounce glasses of milk a day. (One eight-ounce glass of milk supplies 300 milligrams of calcium or 38 percent of the RDA.)

If your child doesn't like milk, you can make sure she gets plenty of calcium by offering cottage cheese, low-fat yogurt, pudding, or American or ricotta cheese. Unless your doctor recommends whole milk, low-fat or skim milk are better choices for children over the age of two.

56

Snacking ruins a child's appetite.

HEALTHY SNACKING IS highly recommended for toddlers and young children. A midmorning and/or a midafternoon snack can prevent a child from getting too hungry and irritable later in the day, and it will give him an energy boost. You can regard snacks as food rather than as treats to be given or withheld based on your child's behavior, and can avoid choosing snacks that are high in fat or cholesterol. Good choices: fruits, vegetables, yogurt, raisins, whole-grain breads, and low-fat cheeses.

A baby should double her birth weight by six months and triple it in a year.

57

FOR AVERAGE BABIES, weighing between seven and eight pounds at birth, this maxim is often true. But if your baby weighed only four pounds at birth, she would almost certainly weigh more than twelve pounds on her first birthday. Conversely, a ten-pounder would be herculean in size if she weighed thirty pounds at the age of one. The ideal growth pattern is one that remains relatively constant, with the weight and height percentiles at comparable levels.

Many babies grow in spurts during the first year, however. So if one measurement seems too low or too high one month, it may not be significant.

SLEEPING

Sleeping in the family bed is good for everyone.

CO-SLEEPING DIVIDES PARENTS, pediatricians, and psychologists into two camps, with proponents noting that babies and small children thrive on the physical closeness it allows, and with critics saying it creates sleep problems for everyone involved. Most authorities agree that past the age of four, children seem better off in their own beds.

There is a very small chance that a parent could roll on top of a young infant, though the likelihood of this is greatly exaggerated. It is best, however, to keep infants off of water beds and soft pillows. Other considerations are more practical than physical: While many women enjoy nursing in bed, keeping the baby in bed afterward may prevent both parents from getting a good night's sleep. Parents need to weigh the pros and cons of the family-bed approach in light of their own lifestyles and beliefs.

Children grow while they're sleeping.

YES, CHILDREN DO GROW when they're sleeping and they grow while they're awake, too. More of the growth hormone is secreted at night, so it is possible that children grow at a somewhat faster rate while they're sleeping, although it's difficult to gauge how much faster.

A cat can jump into a sleeping baby's crib and smother him.

THE THEORY BEHIND THIS myth is that since cats love milk, they'll smell the breast milk or formula on a baby, jump into the crib, sit on the baby's face, and smother him. But no pet, including a cat, can form a complete seal around a baby's mouth and nose and thereby suffocate him.

Parents should introduce the family pet to the new baby slowly and carefully. Dogs, in particular, can become jealous when a newborn arrives on the scene, and some babies may be allergic to dogs or cats right from the start. It's most likely, though, that baby and pet can live happily together under one roof.

Don't let the baby sleep on the same side every night or his head will get flattened.

A MINOR FLATTENING of the head from sleeping in a fixed position can happen with infants, especially with premature babies, whose skulls are somewhat softer. Nearly all full-term babies move around enough when they're sleeping, however, that flattening is rarely an issue. You can alternate the side on which you put your baby to sleep each night if you're concerned. And if your baby's head does get a bit flattened out, don't worry, it will correct itself and round out over the course of several months.

Infants should never sleep on their backs because they could choke.

CONTRARY TO ADVICE from earlier times, sleeping on the back or side is now considered best. For years, pediatricians told parents to put babies to sleep on their stomachs, reasoning that a baby lying on her back could choke if she spit up. Just recently, the American Academy of Pediatrics reversed its stance, and now doctors encourage parents to put babies on their backs or sides. The organization believes there may be a link between infants sleeping on their stomachs and Sudden Infant Death Syndrome (SIDS), the number-one cause of infant death. The pediatricians found no evidence that infants sleeping on their backs are more likely to experience any choking problems.

Parents need not monitor their baby's sleeping position during the night or move her from her stomach to her side. Past the age of six months the risk of SIDS is greatly diminished, so sleeping positions then become less of a concern.

60

Don't let your baby go to sleep with a bottle in his mouth.

A CHILD WHO FALLS ASLEEP with a bottle of milk or juice in his mouth is much more likely to develop baby bottle tooth decay, also called nursing caries. The digestive action of the saliva slows down during sleep so the sugar in the milk and juice has plenty of time to form acids that damage tooth enamel and prompt decay.

To minimize the likelihood of nursing caries, don't let your child take a bottle of milk or juice to bed; brush or wipe his teeth clean after he eats; and put only water in his bedtime bottle past the age of twelve to eighteen months. While nursing caries are far less common in breast-fed babies, they can occur if a baby consistently falls asleep at the breast for long periods of time after his baby teeth come in.

61

A cup of warm milk before bedtime will help your child sleep.

IF DRINKING A CUP of warm milk becomes part of your child's bedtime routine, it probably will help him sleep. But it will work primarily because milk has been associated with bedtime and sleep. If you serve a couple of cookies with the milk, though, you'll enhance his ability to sleep even more because carbohydrates facilitate the body's consumption of tryptophan, a soothing amino acid that's plentiful in milk. Make sure you wipe your child's teeth clean after this snack to avoid tooth decay.

*Don't give in to your child when she doesn't want
to sleep. Let her cry herself to sleep.*

BEDTIME BATTLES ARE the most common problem that
parents of infants, toddlers, and preschoolers voice to their
doctors. During the first year of life, more than 80 percent of
all babies wake up frequently during the night, as do one-third
of all children between the ages of one and five. Half of these
night owls settle back to sleep themselves, but the other half
do not.

Babies under six months of age may still need to be fed
during the night, so letting them "cry it out" is never advised.
For older babies and young children, though, many doctors
advocate this now-popular bedtime approach: Parents spend
two or three minutes comforting their crying child by talking
to her and trying to calm her down without picking her up.
They leave the room and return in ten or fifteen minutes to
comfort her again. They repeat this procedure every night,
increasing the amount of time they let their child cry until
she can sleep on her own. Other sleep-easy strategies include:
establishing a bedtime ritual; providing a comfort object like a
teddy bear or blanket; keeping a night-light on; and supplying
the constant soothing sound of a radio or humidifier.

Your baby should sleep through the night by the time he's three months old.

UNFORTUNATELY, SOME BABIES fail to respond to their parents' desperate pleas for sleep and continue to demand a middle-of-the-night meal long past their third month. Plenty of babies still enjoy those 4 A.M. feedings at five or six months of age. Breast-fed babies often eat more frequently than bottle-fed infants, so they're a bit more likely to wake up because they're hungry. If your baby is six months of age or older and still demanding a night feeding, talk to your pediatrician about ways to train your child to sleep better.

63

If you put a little cereal in your newborn's bottle, he'll sleep through the night.

NO STUDY HAS EVER FOUND a link between early introduction of solids and longer sleeping periods. In fact, offering a child solids too early can predispose him to food allergies and obesity. Contrary to the advice of several generations ago, doctors now recommend holding off on solids—even the seemingly benign rice cereal in a bottle—until a baby is four to six months of age.

You should put your new baby on a strict feeding schedule right away or else she'll take over your lives.

THOUGH YOU MAY BE TIRED of your newborn's insistence on twenty-four-hour room service, you should continue to feed your newborn on demand. Bottle-fed infants generally want to eat every three or four hours, while breast-fed babies like to eat more often since breast milk is more easily digested than formula. While you shouldn't put your new baby on a rigid feeding schedule, you can try to coax a nosher to lengthen the time between meals by playing with her or offering a bottle of water.

64

GENERAL HEALTH
AND WELL-BEING

Propping up a baby can strain her back.

DURING THE FIRST TWO months of life, an infant needs more back and neck support than sitting up provides. Once she's beyond that floppy stage, she can be propped up in a carriage or on a couch. At that point, propping her up won't strain her back and it will probably delight her senses as she gains a whole new perspective on life.

Swaddling a newborn in a blanket will keep her back straight.

SWADDLING WON'T KEEP her back straight but it will make her feel warm and secure. Many newborns like being wrapped tightly in a soft blanket because it reminds them of the close quarters of their first home—the womb. While swaddling can entice many babies to sleep better and protect them from drafts, some of the young and restless don't like their movements restricted quite so much. Follow your baby's cues and cease swaddling when your baby is a month old so she can start kicking.

The night air is bad for babies.

NO EVIL SPIRITS OR TOXINS are lurking in the night air. Since it's colder at night, however, you do need to be sure your baby is dressed appropriately, and you may want to skip night outings if it's rainy, windy, or particularly cold. During the first year of life a baby's internal temperature control isn't fully matured, so it's best to dress him in layers that you can peel off or add to as the temperature dictates. One general guideline is to dress your baby as you are dressed and then add one more layer of clothing.

66

You shouldn't take a newborn outdoors during the first two weeks of life.

IF YOU'RE FEELING up to it, short field trips during the first two weeks will do both you and your baby good. Just make sure your baby is dressed warmly—but not overdressed—and protected from direct sunlight. And since newborns are highly susceptible to infections during the first month of life, it's best to limit your baby's exposure to crowds.

Don't let strangers handle your newborn.

THIS IS PROBABLY good advice. The most common risk from contact with strangers is exposure to infection, particularly during a newborn's first month when her immune system is still developing. It's certainly your prerogative to ask anyone—including friends and relatives—to wash their hands before they touch the baby. Just because someone you meet on the street or in the grocery store asks to hold or touch the baby, you don't need to feel compelled to hand her over.

On the other hand, the world loves a baby. Once your baby is six weeks old or so you may not need to adopt such a strong "hands off" policy with people you don't know well but instinctively trust.

Don't let a child chew gum or it will stick to her stomach.

GUM WON'T STICK to her stomach, but it does pose a choking hazard. Since gum is indigestible, it travels straight through the digestive tract. Along the way, it can lodge in a child's narrow throat. For this reason, gum is not recommended for a child under the age of five.

*If your child has a cold or the flu, give her
baby aspirin.*

FOR YEARS, PARENTS USED baby aspirin to combat their child's fever or flu symptoms. But doctors rescinded this advice when studies in the early 1980s revealed that aspirin is associated with Reye syndrome in children. This rare liver condition can cause brain damage and prove fatal if untreated. For that reason, aspirin is not recommended for anyone under the age of twenty-one. Doctors now recommend acetaminophen as the best cold or flu medicine for children.

*Once your child attends a day-care center or
nursery school, she'll catch cold after cold.*

UNFORTUNATELY, this observation is true. While a young child may average three to five colds a year, once she enters a program with other children she's more likely to catch five to ten colds a year. As she mingles with more children, she increases her exposure to various illnesses. And since toddlers tend to sneeze and cough directly into the faces of their playmates, colds are spread rapidly from one youngster to another. This rampant passing of germs seems to peak among children eighteen months of age.

The good news is that according to new studies, children who had a lot of colds as preschoolers develop immunities and may have fewer colds after they enter elementary school.

If you're a nervous mother, your baby will be colicky.
Only inexperienced parents have colicky babies.

ALTHOUGH THEORIES ABOUND about why some babies develop colic, the two assertions that a nervous mother or inexperienced parents cause colic have no basis in fact. Second-born children are just as likely to develop colic as firstborn babies are. And if a nervous mother were to blame, why would her baby cry only at certain times of the day and be content the rest of the time? Why wouldn't his sobs subside when dad took over? It is true that a baby can sense his parent's unease, though, so staying calm may help the situation.

Once you've eliminated the possibility that your baby is allergic to his formula or to something in your diet if you're nursing, it's best to focus on the treatments for colic rather than on its possible causes. Ask your doctor about soothing techniques, such as drops that prevent gas pains with meals, or other medicine that may help alleviate the discomfort.

69

Babies cry to exercise their lungs.

BABIES CRY TO COMMUNICATE their wants and needs. Crying is how they let their parents know that they're hungry, tired, wet, cold, or in need of a hug. Four out of five infants do, however, have nightly crying bouts that are unrelated to their basic needs. As babies get older, they (thankfully) cry less and are more easily soothed.

Going outdoors with wet hair, sleeping in a draft, or staying outside too long in cold air will give a baby a cold.

THERE'S ONLY ONE WAY to catch a cold and that's by picking up a virus from someone else. Most colds are spread via germ-laden droplet spray in the air, but some are caused by direct contact with the germs. When adults or children infected with one of the two-hundred known viruses cough, sneeze, or touch their eyes or nose, they spread these germs on the surfaces around them, where others pick them up and catch an infection.

While staying out—with wet or dry hair—in cool weather won't give you a cold, most colds do occur in winter. This increase is attributed to the fact that we spend more time indoors during winter months and come into closer contact with sick people. And while sitting in a draft won't cause a cold, in some sensitive people it can trigger a stuffy, runny nose. The cold air can cause blood vessels in the mucous membranes of the nose to swell and release moisture.

Newborns are immune to colds.

WHILE BABIES ARE BORN WITH certain immunities, this is not one of them. And because babies are often kissed on the mouth and touched on the hands by adoring relatives, they're constantly exposed to germs. Even mild colds are particularly distressing to newborns since they breathe primarily through their noses. It's not until they're about three months of age that they completely master breathing through their mouths. Parents can use a bulb syringe or saltwater nose drops to keep baby's nasal passages clear.

Feed a cold and starve a fever.

71

THIS VERY COMMON MAXIM is actually bad advice. A child's appetite, particularly an infant's, normally decreases during the course of a cold, so it's better not to force her to eat. Too much food may even lead to an upset stomach or diarrhea. When a child is feverish, you shouldn't withhold food from her. Offer her a variety of foods and let her eat what she wants. While she may not be as hungry as usual, the food she does eat will help her fight off her infection.

With either a cold or a fever, a child may become dehydrated, so you should concentrate on feeding her liquids, particularly water and juice. Saltwater nose drops administered before meals can temporarily clear nasal passages and enable her to eat or drink more comfortably.

A child can't get a sunburn on a cloudy day.

EVEN ON A CLOUDY DAY, 60 to 80 percent of the sun's harmful ultraviolet rays can reach your child. To protect him, limit his exposure to the sun between 10 A.M. and 2 P.M. (eleven and three during daylight savings time), when the sun is strongest. Keep exposure at any time to a minimum for babies under one. For babies over six months, particularly if you live in a warm climate, apply a sunscreen year-round; look for one that's hypoallergenic and has a sun protection factor (SPF) of 15 or more.

Children need plenty of sunshine so they can get vitamin D.

72

VITAMIN D IS IMPORTANT during infancy because it enhances a baby's bone development, and sunshine stimulates vitamin D production in the body. On the other hand, too much exposure to the sun can be harmful (see above). The babies most at risk for a vitamin D deficiency are those who are breast-fed, since nearly all formulas are vitamin D–fortified.

Moderate exposure to the sun—an average of two hours a week for a fully clothed white infant and only thirty minutes a week for an infant in diapers—is all it takes for a baby's body to produce enough vitamin D. Black and brown-skinned babies need to stay in the sun a little longer since their darker skin takes longer to absorb the sun's rays.

Don't bathe a newborn in a tub before the umbilical cord has fallen off; the water could run into his body and drown him.

YOU CAN WASH A NEWBORN but you shouldn't immerse him in the tub, though the reason has nothing to do with a leaky cord. The stump of the umbilical cord isn't an open hole through which water can run into the body, but it is a common entry point for infection. To keep the area clean, parents can give their newborn a sponge bath and dab the stump with alcohol four or five times a day until the cord falls off, sometime in the first two weeks.

Tickling a baby's feet will make him a stutterer.

IF HE'S LAUGHING and trying to talk at the same time, he may have a hard time speaking. But tickling causes no harm to the baby and he's sure to love it.

Encourage your baby to use her right hand so she'll become right-handed.

MOST CHILDREN ARE ambidextrous until the age of three or four. As early as four months, though, you can sometimes get a clue whether your child will be right- or left-handed by seeing which hand she favors when reaching for objects.

It's never advisable to encourage a child who's naturally left-handed to become right-handed, or vice versa. About 6 to 8 percent of the population are lefties.

73

Children will outgrow their allergies.

SOME DO, some don't. Twenty-five percent of children with food allergies outgrow them after avoiding the known allergens for one to two years. Fifty percent of asthmatic children permanently outgrow the condition, while 25 percent temporarily outgrow it but then experience the symptoms again in adulthood. Early cases of eczema generally clear up by the time children turn five. Pollen allergies, however, often do not surface until late childhood or early adulthood.

Dangling a toy too close to a baby's face will give her crossed eyes.

74

CROSSING OF THE EYES has nothing to do with how near or far a toy is dangled in front of the baby's face. A toy or object held eighteen inches from her face is at an optimal focusing distance. During the first weeks of life, a baby's flat nose and surrounding skin folds may make her eyes look crossed when they're not. In other instances, an infant's eyes may not work in unison and temporarily cross. This tendency disappears within the first few months. As an infant develops the ability to track objects, her eyes may temporarily cross as the object moves closer to her face. About 5 percent of all children do have crossed or wandering eyes, which can usually be corrected.

Thumb-sucking causes buck teeth and ruins the shape of the mouth.

THUMB-SUCKING UP TO the age of four is considered normal and harmless. At least half of all children reportedly suck their thumbs until the age of three. A child who sucks his thumb until the age of four may push his front baby teeth forward and his lower teeth backward, but this shouldn't affect the placement or alignment of the adult teeth, which start coming in at about six years of age. Frequent thumb-sucking after the fourth birthday, however, can affect the permanent alignment of the adult teeth.

Parents should not chastise a child who sucks his thumb nor try to use any devices designed to squelch the habit. Unless parents make a big deal about their child's thumb-sucking, the habit rarely persists beyond the age of four.

If your baby gets diaper rash, extra water will cure it.

UNDER CERTAIN CIRCUMSTANCES, giving your baby extra water can help clear up diaper rash. If, for instance, your baby's been drinking little or no water, his urine may become too concentrated and acidic. That's when extra water can help. Adding too much water or other liquids to his diet, however, can lead to excessive urination, which can exacerbate the problem. To help cure diaper rash—which is quite common and peaks around eight months—air dry your baby's bottom, avoid rubber pants, wash the area gently, and use liberal amounts of antirash ointment.

If you don't wean your baby from a bottle by eighteen months, you'll have a hard time breaking your child's dependency on it.

IT'S TRUE THAT a toddler who cherishes his "ba ba" is not going to give it up easily and may want it by his side and in his mouth long past his second birthday. But what's the big deal? He's not going to arrive at his college dorm with a bottle in tow. Having a bottle constantly in his mouth can promote baby bottle tooth decay, though (see page 61). If weaning your child from a bottle by twelve to eighteen months seems impossible, you can try to avoid tooth decay by putting only water in his bottle and cleaning his teeth after every feeding.

PHYSICAL AND INTELLECTUAL DEVELOPMENT

A child shouldn't wear shoes before she can walk.

A child's first shoe should be the traditional, high-topped leather variety.

A CHILD DOESN'T NEED shoes indoors either before or after she starts walking—in fact, going barefoot enhances muscular development and helps her learn how to walk. If occasionally you want to dress up your pre-walking baby with shoes, go ahead, just make sure the shoes have soft, flexible soles and are made of breathable material, like leather or canvas, not plastic or vinyl.

When shopping for toddler shoes, look for good treading, a flexible sole, a slight heel, and a firm back to the shoe. Both sneakers and the high-topped leather variety work well but sandals fall off too easily. The most important factor in buying shoes for a child is selecting a pair that fits right. Since a child's feet can grow three or four sizes between the ages of one and two, it's important to check fit frequently, every four to eight weeks. After she is three years old, her foot grows less rapidly and requires a shoe-fit check every four to six months.

If a baby doesn't wear shoes when he first walks, he'll become flat-footed.

AT BIRTH, AN INFANT usually has flat feet. Whether he wears shoes when he first walks, or whether he walks early or late will have no impact on this condition.

By the time a child turns three, his feet probably won't look flat any longer; the protective layer of fat that concealed the arch in his foot will have disappeared.

If you push a child to walk too early, he'll become bowlegged.

NEITHER STANDING NOR WALKING early causes bowleg-gedness, which is actually a normal characteristic of babies under two. Most toddlers will look bowlegged until they're about two and a half, at which point they tend to overcorrect their gait and appear knock-kneed. A child's legs generally straighten out completely by the time he's five.

Besides, it's futile to try to push your baby to walk early, since he'll walk only when he's ready to. Sixty percent of babies walk by their first birthdays, with some beginning as early as nine or ten months. Others may wait until they're eighteen months old to take their first steps.

All newborns are born with blue eyes.

THE EYES OF FAIR-SKINNED babies are dark blue or gray-blue at birth. Asians and darker-skinned infants, however, have brown eyes when they're born. By about the sixth month of life, a baby's eyes will have changed color and become their permanent shade of blue, brown, or green. Until then, a baby's eyes can change color by the day or even by the hour.

Newborns are color blind.

WHILE PARENTS MAY DECORATE the nursery in pastels, newborns have a distinct preference for black-and-white pictures, high-contrast patterns, and the brightness of the color red. But it's not until four months of age that an infant's color vision is fully matured. Until then, she has a hard time distinguishing similar colors or shades of the same color.

Newborns can't see at birth.

INFANTS CAN SEE AT BIRTH, but with 20/200 vision the
world appears a bit blurry at first. The lens of a newborn's eyes
doesn't change shape to focus on objects at different distances;
his focus range is preset at eight to eighteen inches in front of
him. A newborn is also extremely sensitive to bright lights, and
he will track moving faces and objects in front of him. His
favorite visual attraction is the human face. By four months
of age, he can distinguish one face from another and show
his preference for the familiar faces of mom and dad.

Walkers help a baby learn to walk earlier.

A WALKER—an oval, wheeled support system that adjusts to
let the baby's feet just reach the floor—can sometimes lessen a
baby's motivation to walk since it enables her to get around so
easily. While walkers can also strengthen calf muscles, they do
not develop the buttocks or thigh muscles, which are used
most during walking.

Pediatricians often advise against the use of walkers
because they can tip over, tumble down stairs, or run into furniture at high speeds. Keeping an eye on your baby when she's
in a walker and balancing the time she spends trundling with
time spent on other activities can make walkers safer and more
enjoyable.

TV helps children learn to talk.

CERTAIN EDUCATIONAL PROGRAMS like "Sesame Street" and "Mister Rogers' Neighborhood" can help a child learn language, particularly when you watch the program too and reinforce what she's seeing and hearing. But constantly plopping a child in front of a television can actually hinder language development and inhibit exercise. The best way to help your child learn language is to describe the goings-on in her daily life, identify objects when she's interested in them, and read to her.

Children who speak early are brighter than others.

EARLY SPEAKERS MAY OR MAY NOT be brighter since few hard-and-fast rules pertain to language development. One- and two-year-olds who acquire language skills slowly may still be whiz kids down the road. Einstein, for example, reportedly didn't utter a word till he was three.

DISCIPLINE AND CHILD REARING

Once a baby starts using a pacifier, he'll never want to give it up.

Give a baby a pacifier and he won't suck his thumb.

PLENTY OF BABIES give up their beloved pacifiers on their own during their first year of life, while others want to hold on to them well into toddlerhood. By the time a child reaches pre-school, peer pressure will usually convince him to abandon sucking his pacifier or thumb in public.

Children do seem to choose either to use a pacifier or to suck their thumbs, and there are pros and cons to each soothing device. Thumbs are free, they don't get lost, and they're more hygienic than pacifiers. On the other hand, pacifiers are orthodontically designed and easier to wean from a child. If you have a strong aversion to pacifiers, you can choose not to introduce one or else take it away from your baby by three or four months of age, before he's developed a strong attachment to it.

Don't pick up the baby every time he cries or you'll spoil him!

THIS MAY BE the one piece of unsolicited advice new parents hear most often. Babies can't be spoiled for at least the first six months of life. When your infant is crying, he generally has a physical or emotional need only you can help him meet. If you respond to his replies quickly, you'll actually help him evolve into a happy, trusting, more self-reliant child, one who will cry less in the long run.

After around seven months, however, babies can start to manipulate their parents. As long as your child's physical needs are being met and he receives plenty of attention from a loving parent or caregiver, you don't need to hold your baby all day long.

83

Spare the rod, spoil the child.

ALTHOUGH SPANKING has been used as a form of discipline for generations, it is now considered inappropriate. Spanking rarely persuades a child to give up bad behavior, and it sends a powerful and harmful message about the acceptable use of violence. There are other ways to discipline a child. Using "time-outs" or intervening quickly to minimize battles between siblings or peers are better approaches to discipline.

If your child bites you, bite her back.

UNDER NO CIRCUMSTANCES should you bite your child. It conveys the message that inflicting pain is OK, exactly what you don't want to communicate.

Biting is not uncommon among toddlers and pre-schoolers. If your child bites another person, remove her from the situation and calmly explain that biting hurts and is unacceptable behavior. It's important to acknowledge her anger and frustration and suggest better ways she can express these feelings, such as shouting "I'm angry" or stomping her feet. Resist the temptation to label your child a "bad girl" and try to lower her frustration level by offering her choices whenever possible. Luckily, the biting phase generally passes by the age of three.

84

Ignore your child's bad behavior and it will go away.

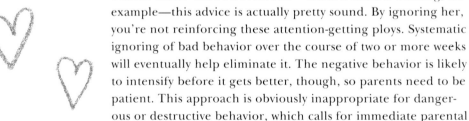

UNDER MANY CIRCUMSTANCES—when a child is whining, for example—this advice is actually pretty sound. By ignoring her, you're not reinforcing these attention-getting ploys. Systematic ignoring of bad behavior over the course of two or more weeks will eventually help eliminate it. The negative behavior is likely to intensify before it gets better, though, so parents need to be patient. This approach is obviously inappropriate for dangerous or destructive behavior, which calls for immediate parental intervention.

If your baby gets upset when you leave him, you should sneak out so he won't know you're gone.

TEMPORARILY AVOIDING separation anxiety may seem less painful for both of you but it can be more harmful in the long run. If you sneak out and don't announce your departure, your baby may worry that you can disappear at any time. Instead, tell your child in advance that you're going out and then make as little fuss as possible when you leave. Always reassure your child that you'll be back.

Some parents find a goodbye ritual—a special kiss or storytime beforehand—can help ease separation anxiety, which generally peaks between ten and eighteen months of age. Whenever you drop your child off with a sitter or at a day-care center, spend a little time with him before you leave.

85

*Don't leave a baby with a sitter until she's
one year old.*

FORTUNATELY FOR PARENTS, this highly impractical advice
is unnecessary. It's not whether a child has a full-time sitter
before the age of one but rather the quality of the care, the
child's temperament, and the "goodness of fit" between the
baby and caregiver that matter. Other important factors influ-
encing the baby's emotional development are the level of
stress in the home and the parents' attitude about leaving the
child, either for work or a "date." Even the most devoted parents need to spend time away from their child on occasion.

86

*The best way to deal with "stranger anxiety"
is to introduce your baby to new people.*

STRANGER ANXIETY, a fear of unfamiliar people, often
surfaces around six months of age. It's a positive development
since it shows that your baby has created a mental image of the
people she's most familiar with. You can try to minimize the
extent of her distress in advance by introducing her to a wide
range of people early on.

GENDER AND BIRTH-ORDER DIFFERENCES

Boys are more physically active than girls.

RIGHT FROM THE START, boys are more aggressive physically than girls. Higher levels of the male hormone testosterone predispose boys to aggression. In general, boys are more active and exploratory than girls and like group play while girls prefer one-on-one interaction. Girls also seem to have more impulse control and higher tolerance for frustration.

Some of these early contrasts have a physiological basis, but social conditioning and cultural expectations play a large role in creating gender differences as well. Don't worry if your daughter demonstrates some "male" traits or your son some "female" ones. After all, it's the special blending of different traits that makes each of us unique and interesting.

Girls look like their fathers and boys resemble their mothers.

NOT NECESSARILY. In your family, the adorable little girl may look like daddy and the cute little boy may resemble mommy, but since physical characteristics are determined by a random mixing of dominant and recessive genes, there is no pattern for all families.

Girls learn to speak faster than boys.

YOUNG GIRLS DO, in fact, have a three to four month advantage over boys in the acquisition of language, particularly between eighteen months and three years of age, when children are first learning to speak. Even through elementary school, girls often retain more extensive vocabularies than boys. By adolescence, there's virtually no difference between the sexes in verbal communication skills.

Boys should only play with trucks and girls with dolls.

WHETHER A BOY PLAYS with a doll or a truck will have no impact on his sexual orientation. But insisting that he play only with trucks and soldiers can make him feel guilty and anxious when he wants to play with a doll. Playing with a doll can also help a young boy be nurturing and express tenderness. Similarly, insisting that a girl should not play with trucks or soldiers will send her an unnecessary and stereotyped message about limitations and roles.

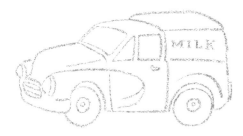

Firstborns are always the smartest.

Middle children feel neglected.

The youngest child in the family is always the most spoiled.

ACCORDING TO BIRTH-ORDER theorists, firstborns tend to be the biggest achievers, getting the highest test scores and landing the most prestigious jobs. Such world-class achievers as Sandra Day O'Connor, Margaret Mead, and Bill Cosby fall into this category. On the other hand, many other super-achievers were not the first child. Bobby Kennedy, Walt Disney, and Margaret Thatcher were second or middle children, while Barbara Walters, Pope John Paul II, and Jackie Robinson were the babies in their families.

It's true that a firstborn gets her parents to herself for a time, while middle children and later-borns have to share them from day one. But then parents may be more relaxed with their children after the first, since they've been through many of the traumas and joys before. Birth order alone is not a reliable predictor of a child's personality or future success, and besides, the family dynamic changes with each child. Parents can make each child feel special by not comparing one child to another and by focusing on each of their individual characteristics and talents.

Older women are more likely to have twins.

A WOMAN OVER THIRTY is four times more likely than a younger woman to have fraternal twins. The reason: Her ovaries are more likely to release more than one egg at a time. Also, the more pregnancies she's had, the more likely she is to have fraternal twins. Race, too, plays a role: Black women are much more likely to conceive fraternal twins than white women, who are more likely to bear twins than are Asians. Tall or overweight women are also more likely to have twins. Those with the highest chance of multiple births, though, are women taking fertility drugs.

These factors play no role in a woman's chances of having identical twins, which form when one fertilized egg divides in half. One-third of all twins are identical.

Twins run in families.

FRATERNAL TWINS, but not identical twins, run in families. A woman with one pair is four times more likely to have twins again, and if she's a twin herself, her chances of twinning are twice the average. This hereditary link appears only in the mother's family, however, not the father's.

RELATIONSHIPS

If you don't bond with your baby immediately after birth, you never will.

BONDING IS JUST NOT that fast and simple. Parent-child bonding is a complicated emotional process that takes months or years to evolve. Some mothers worry—unnecessarily—that they won't bond because they weren't able to hold their babies immediately after birth. Other moms and dads worry that they just don't "feel connected" or don't "feel the way they should" when they first see their newborn. What molds the parent-child relationship is not this instantaneous love but rather the strong attachment that develops over time and is sustained throughout life.

Don't change your perfume or your baby won't recognize you.

THE SENSE OF SMELL is highly refined in a newborn even within the first forty-eight hours of life. Newborns can distinguish the smell of their mother's breast milk from other milk within the first week of life. While a baby can associate the smell of a certain perfume or hand lotion with his mother, even if she switches scents he'll still be able to recognize her face, voice, and touch.

Once you have a child, forget about sex.

THE DEMANDS OF A NEW BABY can make it temporarily challenging to find enough time and energy for sex, but the world's middle children and later-borns are proof that it can be done. Think creatively about romantic touches—flowers, a massage, a little gift—that remind your partner that you still find him (or her) special. As soon as you're comfortable leaving your baby with a sitter, try designating one evening a week as your "night out" without the baby, even if you sometimes wind up sequestering yourselves in the bedroom.

92

The best gift parents can give their child is a strong marriage.

HAVING A STRONG MARRIAGE helps your child in many ways: It provides a role model for a healthy relationship; it ensures that the two people who love her most remain involved in her daily life; and it enhances her sense of security. Seeing that your marriage stays strong will help the entire family.

If there's a three-year gap between children, you won't have to deal with sibling rivalry.

THEORIES ABOUND about the perfect spacing for happy, peace-loving siblings. (The only constant advice is that women should wait a minimum of three months after delivery before conceiving again so their bodies can bounce back before beginning another pregnancy.) But "ideal" spacing depends largely on the needs and wants of the family, the temperaments of the children involved, and how they're nurtured.

Parents can try to minimize sibling rivalry by finding special traits in each child; encouraging children to settle their disputes peacefully; setting clear limits; and offering plenty of opportunities for cooperation. Sibling rivalry also offers two benefits: It teaches children how to compete fairly and how to stand up for themselves.

93

Boys fall in love with their mothers, and little girls want to marry their fathers.

FREUD WAS RIGHT, there probably will be a moment when your young daughter climbs onto her daddy's lap and says something akin to "Let's dump Mom and go get married." Between the ages of three and six, many if not all children enter the so-called Oedipal (for boys) or Electra (for girls) phase, when they want to remove the same-sex parent and marry the parent of the opposite sex.

When dad's the prize, he should convince his flirtatious daughter that she's attractive but make it clear to her that she will never take mom's place. Mom needs to handle this rejection by her daughter calmly and resist the urge to compete. Along with dad, she needs to assure her daughter that someday her own partner will come. Similarly, parents can gently respond to their son's advances to mom and rejection of dad. Luckily, nearly all children abandon these fantasies by the time they start first grade.

94

Don't dress twins alike or they won't develop separate identities.

WHILE DRESSING TWINS ALIKE may be fun and harmless on occasion, it's better not to treat the children like objects to be adorned instead of two people with separate personalities. Years of being asked by onlookers "which one are you?" does not help anyone's self-esteem or sense of identity.

To help each twin feel special and unique, it's important to avoid comparisons between them and encourage them to have their own sets of friends, toys, and interests. Often, though, twins do enjoy a special relationship with each other throughout their lives.